CLUTTER FREE

CLUTTER FREE

by Leo Babauta and Courtney Carver

Waking Lion Press

ISBN 978-1-4341-0523-3

First published in 2012, this book is uncopyrighted:
https://zenhabits.net/uncopyright/

Published by Waking Lion Press, an imprint of the Editorium

Waking Lion Press™ and Editorium™ are trademarks of:

The Editorium, LLC
West Jordan, UT 84081-6132
www.editorium.com

CONTENTS

INTRODUCTION

Clutter Free is designed to help you remove clutter from your home and your life.

Through three sections you'll uncover the simplest ways to identify the essential and break your attachment to stuff.

Section 1 will help you understand why you've collected the clutter in the first place and why it's so hard to get rid of for good.

Section 2 will show you step by step, and room by room how to get rid of the clutter.

Section 3 will give you ideas to live your new clutter-free life with purpose and joy.

From your junk drawer to your closet, you'll find actionable plans for each space in your home. In addition, you'll learn how to set expectations for gift giving holidays, what clutter-free experiments might help jump start your journey, and how to maintain a new life with more time, space, money and energy.

This book is not about organizing your stuff every January, or the importance of spring cleaning. If you put these recommendations in place, this will be the last time you organize, declutter or have a yard sale.

Part I

EMOTION

learn why and let go

Chapter 1

THE PSYCHOLOGY OF STUFF

The simple action of getting rid of stuff will clear the clutter temporarily, but it might not contribute to a long lasting clutter-free lifestyle. When you lose weight, unless you understand why you were overweight in the first place, and why and how you ate the way you did, the weight will likely creep back on. Similarly, if you jettison your stuff without understanding why you bought it and hold on to it, stuff will creep back in.

Inanimate objects carry great responsibility to fix our lives. Without even knowing it, we depend on our stuff. Examples include:

- the hope chest

- a trust fund

- worry dolls

- a touch stone

While those are the obvious, take a brief inventory of your stuff and ask what you expected of each thing. Did you expect your bed to deliver a great night of sleep? Did you think your computer would make you money? Would your new wine glasses or ice cream maker make you popular?

We've assigned so much power to stuff, that it's become a challenge to let it go. When you let go of stuff, it may feel like you are letting go of hopes and dreams when in reality, you are making room for them. While there are things that can help you accomplish something, you can not depend on stuff. You have to put your trust and faith in people, in yourself, and in God or the Universe or whatever you believe keeps the world spinning.

- When you let go of the idea that the $250 backpack you bought will help you explore the world, you can sell the backpack and start to pay off the debt that is holding you back from traveling.

- When you let go of the idea that the box of exercise equipment sitting in your living room will make you fit, you can dump the guilt and go take a walk, or hike, or do whatever activity you truly enjoy and shift towards a healthier lifestyle.

- When you box up all the clothes that you thought made you look like a professional or any other way that you wanted to be perceived, you can start being who you are, instead of dressing the way you think you are supposed to.

Stuff is just stuff. It's plastic or metal, glass or paper. Each piece of stuff is shaped a little differently, but in the end, it will be in the same donation bin or landfill, likely never having met your expectations.

If you need to place trust in stuff, turn towards the good stuff like gratitude, compassion and happiness. Lean into love and laughter and away from another trip to the mall searching for stuff to change your life.

Chapter 2

THE "JUST IN CASE" SYNDROME

Pay attention to how many times you say "just in case" in one day. You'll be surprised at how often this excuse or reasoning pops up when you are making decisions. From deciding where to live, what to pack on a trip to what to make for dinner, "just in case" is always lurking.

You already know what the "just in case" syndrome is without a lengthy description. You keep things (in your bag, or in your home or office) not because you actually need them, but "just in case."

When we look at this with actual evidence, we see that "just in case" means we keep a lot of stuff we don't actually use. Try an experiment: monitor the "just in case" stuff you pack on a trip, or keep in your home. Make a list of the stuff you keep for "just in case"—stuff you haven't used in the last few months but are worried you might need. Then see how many times in the next 6–9 months you actually use that stuff.

"Just in case" is the reason we hold onto a lot of things. The vast majority of the time, we don't need them. But we're afraid we might, so we hoard. It wards off insecurities about the future. Challenge that theory, let go and see what happens. Experience trumps fear.

Holding on to too much "just in case" is comfortable, but dangerous. We've lived in excess for so long that it becomes hard to recognize what enough really is. The only way to see it is to start letting go. With each layer that you discard, you'll reveal a little bit more about how living with less really does give you more.

"Just in case" has become a popular answer to "why do you need that?" When you take time to finish the "just in case" sentence, you might find that it's not a very good excuse.

Do you really need . . .

- 8 coffee cups "just in case" eight people are all drinking coffee at the same time?

- 3 purses "just in case" the bottom falls out of the one you use now.

- the gold you were going to sell "just in case" the price of gold goes up.

- store credit cards "just in case" you can earn points and buy something you don't need, so you can get something you don't want for free.

- high school jeans,"just in case" 20 pounds disappear in your sleep

Sound familiar? Maybe those questions are a little silly, but think of the number of times you've purchased something or done something "just in case." What are you really worried about?

Without "just in case" you became more confident in your choices and learn that you don't need a back up plan for every decision.

Chapter 3

WHEN STUFF IS SENTIMENTAL

Letting go of stuff that you've attached feelings, memories or expectations to can be challenging. It can also be very rewarding, when you realize that those things don't hold anything that your heart can't hold onto all by itself.

We become attached to things that remind us of our past, and our loved ones. Your great grandfather's pocket watch, your first pair of roller skates, or your son's artwork from kindergarten, all transport you to another time, and usually fill you with lovely memories.

Unfortunately, because you don't want to clutter your home with stuff, these treasures are buried in boxes in the garage or attic, only to be rediscovered during a move, or a trip down memory lane.

How do you get rid of the stuff that means so much, and evokes so much emotion? Here are a few ways to simplify the sentimental.

Show it

Unless you are on a mission to live with less than a certain number of things, why not display some of your sentimental items? Less does not mean none. Paring down your objects of memory does not necessarily mean ridding yourself of them all. Instead focus on the most meaningful items. Chances are, the things with all the memories are in a box in the garage or attic. Sort through those boxes and choose the things that mean most to you and your family and display them.

Sometimes we hold onto things to hold onto people that have left our lives. Honor the ones you love by sharing what was theirs. After all, a box full of memories stashed in the basement is far less meaningful than 3–4 specific items displayed in your home. So go through that box of mother's things in the basement, select the three that best represented her life and the influence that she had, display them proudly, and remove the rest.

Use it

Did you save the china that your parents received on their wedding day or a special necklace that was passed down to you? Why not use it? Donate your everyday plates and eat off the dishes that mean so much. Wear the memorable piece of jewelry every day instead of waiting for a special occasion, or forgetting about it completely. You may come across things that you can't use and don't want to keep, but someone else will find your sentimental items to be quite useful. Use them or pass them on.

Shoot it

When you are decluttering, save the things that mean the most to you, and take a picture before letting them go. Preserve the memories inspired by stuff through photography. Group items creatively or take pictures using the things. For instance, if you saved a baseball hat from your childhood little league team, take a picture of your child wearing it. Create a digital photo book with images and descriptive text, so you can enjoy your memories without the clutter. A book like this makes a beautiful gift to someone else in the family who wants to enjoy the memories without the clutter.

Share it

The most powerful thing we can offer is our story. As you simplify your life, you will come to the realization that the most sentimental things aren't things at all, but stories of the people and places you love, and how you spend our time. Write and talk about the things you love, instead of holding onto them. Start a family blog or keep a personal journal. Your words may start out describing your mother's watch, but turn into a beautiful story about an afternoon the two of you spent together.

When you've lived without your sentimental items, you'll notice that you aren't any less sentimental. You don't care less. In fact, with less clutter, you can reflect on your memories and tell stories from the heart about important times and people.

Chapter 4

For the Love of Stuff

What do you do if you can't let go of something you own?

How do you deal with the "just in case" syndrome, or the "it has meaning" syndrome?

There's no easy answer for letting go of the emotional attachments you put into your objects, nor for letting go of the fear of what you might need in the future unless you change the way you look at ownership.

Start thinking about ownership as something more fluid and less concrete. We don't own something for life—that's wasteful, because we usually don't need or want something for that long. Could you "own" something just for as long as you need it, and then pass it on?

Think of ownership like a public library—we check things out when we need them, and then return them when we're done, so that others can use them. If we ever need something, we can always check it out again.

This means passing books and clothes and other things on to friends and relatives when you don't need them. It means giving things away to Goodwill and other charities. It means getting things from Goodwill, used book stores, thrift shops,

Craigslist, Freecycle, friends and family. And yes, sometimes it means buying things that you owned years before.

Occasionally you will spend a little more, but it also means you are giving away a lot of value, and others benefit from things you think are great. It means things pass through your life, into the lives of others. Instead of hoarding your stuff, you have an opportunity to share it.

This practice will result in objects holding less emotional meaning so the meaning in your life is instead put into experiences, relationships and conversations.

If you need something, you can get it again

If you aren't using something, let someone else use it who might need it. And you'll save yourself a lot of expenses: moving the stuff, storing it, caring for it, mentally remembering everything you have, fixing things that get broken, cleaning things, stressing over how many things you have.

Giving things away is not money down the drain

If you enjoyed a book, don't hold on to it because you spent $10.00. You paid for the enjoyment of the story and not the physical book.

Don't worry about decorative things

When you have emptiness in your home, you have space to fill it with conversation, play, laughter, and silence. When you fill your house with stuff, you do it to stave off the void, to avoid having to fill it with experiences and silence.

There is almost nothing in your life that's
irreplaceable, other than people

And in the end, you learn that the people and the moment
are all that matter.

Everything else comes and goes.

Chapter 5

A BETTER REASON TO BUY

If you've ever purchased something to keep up, measure up, fit in or rise above, then you understand that you don't always buy what you love or what you need. Sometimes you buy what you think you should own based on the actions of others.

Maybe it was a lawn mower that your neighbor had, or a flat screen TV that you enjoyed at your brother's house. They seem happy with the purchase, so maybe it will make you happy too.

The reality is that if you buy to impress or to fill an emotional void, like happiness, the feeling fades faster than you can pay off your credit card.

Reasons you buy now

ADVERTISING

The purpose of a magazine ad, billboard, TV or radio spot is to convince you to take action. Expensive advertising campaigns paint a picture of what businesses want you to expect from a product or service. When you feel swayed, remind yourself that you cannot buy a lifestyle. You can only create one, from the inside out.

SOCIETAL PRESSURE

Everyone else goes to the mall, gets excited about big sales and forwards their Groupon, so to feel normal, so do you. Unfortunately, being normal also comes with too much house, a car you can't afford and hefty debt. As financial expert Dave Ramsey would say, "If that's normal, I want to be weird."

BOREDOM

Boredom comes in many forms including lack of focus, depression and not knowing what you really want. Instead of addressing the issue, it's easier to eat a cheeseburger or buy a new pair of shoes. Next time you recognize boredom or unease, take a walk or write about how you are feeling.

THE PURSUIT OF HAPPINESS

Somehow, we started to believe that happiness can be bought. We confused the rush of getting a good deal with being happy. We thought that the latest and greatest would put us on top of the world and turn our discontentment into joy. In reality, happiness comes from inside, from the way you look at things and from the way you connect with others. Choose real happiness over synthetic joy.

How do you stop the habit of shopping? More importantly, how can you stop from wanting the things that your friends have, or that you read about in a magazine? When you find something more important and more meaningful and can clearly identify it, shopping for sport seems silly. You may never lose that feeling of desire when you walk by your favorite shop, or hear about something new being released, but with contentment, and purpose, you can thoughtfully assess the purchase, instead of shopping mindlessly.

When you decide that time is more important than money and people are more important than things, you can begin to ask the following questions before making a purchase:

- How will I use this?

- How will this add real value to my life?

- Can I borrow it instead?

- Do I need it today?

- Do I need it at all?

If you come to the conclusion after asking the right questions that you really need the item or service, wait 30 days. Time may dull your excitement or need for the purchase.

Buying things is not bad, but buying things for the wrong reason will never result in long term happiness.

Be happy. Be weird.

Chapter 6

IDENTIFY WHAT IS MOST IMPORTANT

Before you begin the process of becoming clutter free, everything seems important and it's hard to know where to start. As you work through each part of your home and life and begin paring down, you will start to see what is most meaningful to you.

Don't focus on why it's taking so long to declutter. Remind yourself that it took you 20, 30, 40 years or more to accumulate your stuff, so it will take some time to free yourself of it.

Before you begin to let go, give some thought to your stuff. Sit down in a room in your house, and look around. Do you use everything around you? Do you love everything around you? Are you still paying for what's around you? Is everything surrounding you worth the hours you put in to pay for it? What about what you pay to insure it or the time you spend taking care of it or just thinking about it?

Once you've assessed the damage, it's time to let go of the guilt so you can let go of the stuff. The natural response to change is to resist and the easiest way to resist is by feeling bad about what you are doing. Don't be surprised as you start to box up the clutter, if you think about some of the following things:

- I spent so much money on that, I should keep it.

- I might need that someday.

- Maybe I should save that to pass down to my children.

Just because you spent money once on something, doesn't mean you need to keep investing in it by keeping it around. Maybe you don't need to keep paying money for your item, but you will continue to pay time and attention if you keep it. Wouldn't you rather use your precious time and attention for something more important?

If you don't know what is more important or most important yet, don't worry. The closer you become to clutter free, the easier it will be to understand what you really care about. By clearing the clutter, you can begin to breathe, to focus and to discover what makes your heart sing.

Chapter 7

GIVE PRESENCE

Have you ever given a gift to demonstrate your love for someone? What about a gift to apologize? Or a present to compensate for time you didn't spend with someone?

A gift for any of those reasons is not bad or wrong, but in each instance, the person you please is usually yourself. The recipient may like the gift, but still may feel like they are missing something.

As you begin to live a clutter-free life, you will notice that you have more time to spend with people that you care about. When you aren't worried about stuff, debt and a jam packed day, you can direct your attention to the things and people that matter most.

The best gifts you can give are your time, interest, love and attention. A heartfelt apology will mean more than a dozen roses everyday.

If you live far away from the people you love, dedicate time via phone or Skype. Send letters and email. Show you care with your heart, instead of your wallet. For friends and family that live close by, invest your time and energy in things that are important to them. Support them through tough times. Celebrate successes and lend a shoulder when they need it the most. While there are designated gift giving holidays, being there when someone truly needs you, is better than anything that comes wrapped in shiny paper.

When you are in a situation that requires gift giving, think about giving experiences instead of stuff. A gift certificate to a local restaurant or spa will be well received without taking up space.

Instead of presents, give presence.

Part II

ACTION

get started, the right time is now

Chapter 8

How to Get Started

There are two general approaches to getting started decluttering, depending on whether you feel incredibly excited or overwhelmed/intimidated.

Some people approach the start of decluttering with an immense enthusiasm, and want to tackle everything at once. This isn't a bad approach, but just realize that if you have the typical amount of clutter, you probably won't be able to clear every space in your home in one go. The best way to start in this case is to set aside a decluttering weekend or a few hours a day for a period of 3–4 days.

Most people are a bit overwhelmed, and the idea of tackling everything at once is way too intimidating. In fact, just getting started can be too intimidating, and so they put it off. The best approach in this case is to start small and take things one bit at a time.

Let's look at both approaches.

Starting small

You don't need to worry about all your clutter when you start—you just need to start. So start very small. You can start with your kitchen counter or table. Pick one space, like a table or counter, and clear it off. Put everything to the side, in a pile. Now go through the pile one item at a time, and make a decision, putting things in three piles: keep, toss, or maybe. The keep items should only be things you've used in the last six months and really need, and they need to find a permanent home, probably not on the clear surface you've just created. The toss items should be recycled, donated or trashed. The "maybe" pile is for things you just can't give up at the moment, but haven't used in the last six months—put them in a box for storage, and check back in another six months. If you haven't used them by then, you don't need them.

This session can be done in 10 minutes, if you make quick decisions. And then you have a clear space. Marvel at this space—it's lovely. From this clutter-free center, start moving outward and clearing more space, one flat surface at a time. You don't need to do it all at once—10 minutes a day, and you'll have seven clear surfaces by the end of a week, and 30 by the end of one month. Start small, and increase gradually.

Starting big

If you have the energy and are ready to commit to a big overhaul, then by all means, dive in! It's best to schedule an entire weekend, or if that's not possible then try for 2–4 hours for 2–4 days. Schedule a big block or blocks of time, and declutter as much of your home or office as possible. Do one room at a time. Within each room, do one space at a time—the closet, a shelf, a counter, a part of the floor.

Clear out each space individually, putting everything in a pile and working through it as in the "Start Small" section above. When you've cleared that one space, go to the next. Working quickly, you can do a room in a couple hours (possibly a bit longer if you have a massive amount of stuff).

You probably won't be able to do everything in your home in one go. Realize that you've spent years accumulating this stuff, so it won't get out overnight. You'll probably need time to haul everything out, donating some to charity, giving others to family and friends, and recycling the rest if possible. But with a big chunk of time, you can get a lot done. You'll feel amazing, and be ready to tackle the rest either in small steps (as in Starting Small above), or in another big chunk or two.

Other easy ways to get started when you find a spare 10–20 minutes (no need to do them all at once!):

Designate a spot for incoming papers

Papers often account for a lot of our clutter. This is because we put them in different spots—on the counter, on the table, on our desk, in a drawer, on top of our dresser, in our car. No wonder we can't find anything! Designate an in-box tray or spot in your home (or at your office, for that matter) and don't put down papers anywhere but that spot. Got mail? Put it in the inbox. Got school papers? Put them in the inbox. Receipts, warranties, manuals, notices, flyers? In the inbox! This one little change can really transform your paperwork.

Start clearing a starting zone

What you want to do is clear one area. This is your no-clutter zone. It can be a counter, or your kitchen table, or the three-foot perimeter around your couch. Wherever you start, make a rule: nothing can be placed there that's not actually in use. Everything must be put away. Once you have that clutter-free zone, keep it that way! Now, each day, slowly expand your no-clutter zone until it envelops the whole house!

Pick up five things, and find places for them

These should be things that you actually use, but that you just seem to put anywhere, because they don't have good places. If you don't know exactly where things belong, you have to designate a good spot. Take a minute to think it through—where would be a good spot? Then always put those things in those spots when you're done using them. Do this for everything in your home, a few things at a time.

Spend a few minutes visualizing the room

How would you like the room to look? What are the most essential pieces of furniture? What doesn't belong in the room but has just gravitated there? What is on the floor (hint: only furniture and rugs belong there) and what is on the other flat surfaces? Once you've visualized how the room will look uncluttered, and figured out what is essential, you can get rid of the rest.

Put a load in your car for charity

If you've decluttered a bunch of stuff, you might have a "to donate" pile that's just taking up space in a corner of your room. Take a few minutes to box it up and put it in your trunk. Then tomorrow, drop it off.

Pull out some clothes you don't wear

As you're getting ready for work, and going through your closet for something to wear, spend a few minutes pulling out ones you haven't worn in a few months. If they're seasonal clothes, store them in a box. Get rid of the rest. Do this a little at a time until your closet (and then your drawers) only contains stuff you actually wear.

Clear out your medicine cabinet

If you don't have one spot for medicines, create one now. Go through everything for the outdated medicines, the stuff you'll never use again, the dirty-looking bandages, the creams that you've found you're allergic to, the ointments that never had an effect on your energy or your eye wrinkles. Simplify to the essential.

Pull everything out of a drawer

Just take the drawer out and empty it on a table. Then sort the drawer into three piles: 1) stuff that really should go in the drawer; 2) stuff that belongs elsewhere; 3) stuff to get rid of. Clean the drawer out nice, then put the stuff in the first pile back neatly and orderly. Deal with the other piles immediately!

Learn to love the uncluttered look

Once you've gotten an area decluttered, you should take the time to enjoy that look. It's a lovely look. Make that your standard! Learn to hate clutter! Then catch clutter and kill it wherever it crops up.

Chapter 9

DECLUTTERING AS ZEN MEDITATION

Decluttering your home or workspace can often seem over-whelming, but in truth it can be as peaceful as medita-tion, and can be a way to practice living mindfully and in the moment.

Decluttering can be your zazen, if you approach it from the right mindset. Don't look at it as a big hassle—see it as a way to find a peace of mind.

A few important things to know about clutter

1. Clutter is a manifestation of a) holding onto the past and b) fear of what might happen in the future.

2. Letting go of clutter is a way to live more mindfully and in the present.

3. The act of decluttering itself can be a mindfulness practice.

Let's talk about each of those things briefly.

Clutter is holding onto the past, or fear of the future

Why do we have clutter in the first place? Why do we keep it when we don't really need it? Maybe we think we do need it—for two reasons:

1. WE DON'T WANT TO LET GO OF THE PAST

Often clutter comes in the form of emotional attachment to objects that have significance to us. They might remind us of a loved one, or a vacation, or a special event like a birthday, funeral, graduation, etc. It might be a gift from someone. All of this is living in the past. That's not to say we should forget about the past, but letting go of these objects (and they're only objects, they're not the events or loved ones themselves) . . . it is a way of releasing our hold on the past. It's a way of living more in the present. You don't have to forget the past, but you also don't need to dwell on it.

2. WE'RE AFRAID OF THE FUTURE

Clutter might be things we think we might need sometime in the future. We hold on to them just in case. Over-packing for a trip is a good example—we bring more than we really need, just in case we need them. It's the same in our houses—we have a ton of things we don't really need or use, just in case. We're afraid of being unprepared for the future, but the truth is we can never be totally prepared. We can't control the outcome of the future, and trying to do so means that we're never really living in the present moment. We're always preparing for what might (or might not) come.

Look at your clutter carefully, one object at a time, and ask yourself why you're holding onto each object. It's probably for one of these two reasons, if you're honest.

Btw, books are usually examples of one of these two reasons. We hold onto books we've already read, as trophies of our reading accomplishments. We hold onto books we might read in the future (but probably won't), with the optimism that our future selves are going to be more amazing readers than we've ever been in the past. In truth, you only need three or four books—the ones you might read in the next month. Then after you've read those, donate those books to charity, and check out a few books from the library.

Let go of clutter to live mindfully

So if clutter is holding onto the past, and fearing the future . . . how can we live in the present instead?

If you slowly get rid of clutter, you can release your mind of these attachments and fears. It's a liberating process. Clutter is the physical embodiment of these attachments and fears—emotional stuff that we don't realize we have. By decluttering, we are clearing ourselves of these tangled webs.

And when you've gotten rid of clutter, you're freed. You can forget about those things, and live instead in this moment. You can fully appreciate life as it happens, instead of looking back on what has happened before, or looking forward to what might happen later.

It's of course possible to live in the moment even if you have clutter. There is no prerequisite to mindful living. But decluttering can be a beautiful process of helping ourselves let go of the things we don't realize we're holding on to.

Clutter as mindfulness practice

And so, as you declutter, not only are you freeing yourself up to live in the present . . . you can live in the present during the process of decluttering.

It's a form of zazen—which is sitting meditation, but at its core zazen is really a way to practice being mindful. It's a way to prepare us for dealing mindfully with the rest of the things we do in life. And really, anything can be used as a way to practice mindfulness—running, washing dishes, folding laundry.

And decluttering is one of the best mindfulness practices. Here's how to do it:

Pick one cluttered flat surface

It can be a tabletop, counter top, shelf, the top of a dresser, floor of a closet, floor of a room (just a section of that floor to start with). Don't worry about all the rest of your cluttered spaces for now—just pick this one space. Small is good.

Clear that surface

Take everything off and pile it on the floor or another table. Clean the surface while it's clear—wipe it with a cloth, slowly and mindfully.

Take one object from the pile

Forget about the entire pile—just look at that one object. Ask yourself why you have it. Is it for emotional reasons, or do you really use it? Is it for "just in case"? When was the last time you used it? If you don't really need or use it, put it in a box for donation or trash it. If you do really use it, put it in another pile to be put back on your now-clean surface. If you're on the fence and can't bear to give something up, put it in a "maybe" box and put that box away for six months (mark the date on your calendar).

Repeat, one object at a time

Practice doing this mindfully. Make a decision with each object—keep, donate, or maybe box. No waffling or putting off decisions. Deal with each object once, then move on.

Put the objects back, and make a "home" for each one

Each object needs to have a spot that is its home, and you should always put those objects back in their homes. If you can't find a home for an object, you don't have space for it. Donate the items in the donation box, and put away the maybe box. Eventually you won't need a maybe box as you get good at this.

Learn to focus on one thing at a time, mindfully, and deal with each object once. This is a good practice for doing things in the rest of your life.

Chapter 10

Closets

Even if you don't have a daily routine, you probably visit your closet at least once a day. A sure sign of excess is a closet full of clothes that you don't wear. If you have fat clothes and skinny clothes, tags still hanging on clothing you bought last month, or have ever looked in your closet and thought, "I have nothing to wear," then this is the best place to start working towards your clutter-free life.

The best way to clear out your closet is to literally clear out your closet. Consider your closet to be anywhere you store clothes.

Three Steps to a clutter-free closet

1. Put all of your clothes on your bed. All of them.
2. Divide clothing into 4 piles

- Pile One: I love these items. They fit me well and I wear them frequently: Keep

- Pile Two: I want to keep this but I don't know why
•Pile Three: These items don't fit me or my style: donate.

- Pile Four: These items aren't in good condition: trash.

3. Distribute the piles

  - Take Pile Four to the trash.

  - Box up Pile Three and put in your car before you have time to rethink.

  - Put the items from Pile One back in your closet.

  - Box up all items from Pile Two and put the box in the back of your closet for 30 days.

  - If you didn't miss the box after 30 days, do not open it, donate it.

You might be used to cleaning out your closet seasonally or at least once a year. If you are ruthless with the steps above, you can eliminate the need to constantly organize your clothing. If that is not reason enough to simplify your wardrobe, here are six more ways that dressing with less can improve your life.

1. **Be ready on time.** With fewer options, you'll get ready faster.

2. **Shop less.** After you've cleaned out your closet and made room for your favorite pieces, you'll feel comfortable wearing them. By focusing on simple, classic pieces, you won't have to shop for the latest trend.

3. **Look better.** By dressing with less, you will develop a personal style. Most people don't notice or remember what you are wear, but they will notice when you wear clothing that fits and compliments your body.

4. **Maintain a healthy weight.** Clothes won't help you cut calories, but if you only have one size available, instead of a "fat" section and "skinny" section, you will be more inspired to maintain a healthy weight.

5. **More time.** When you stop spending time thinking about what you are going to wear, trying on outfit after outfit, and regularly shopping for clothes, you'll create more time.

6. **More money.** Less time shopping for clothes and accessories naturally means more money in your bank account. With fewer items, you'll also spend less taking care of them.

Fashion is art and dressing with less doesn't mean that you don't get to appreciate art. If you are inspired by the beauty of fashion, continue to be inspired. You can love the art of Van Gogh without hanging one of his paintings in your living room, so you can admire a Diane Von Furstenberg wrap dress or a pair of Jimmy Choo shoes without putting them in your closet.

If you only keep the clothes that you wear and love, you will dress better and faster. Instead of agonizing over what to wear, you can dedicate your time and energy to things that really matter.

Chapter 11

CONQUER THE JUNK DRAWER

This chapter is not about organizing your junk drawer. This is about getting rid of your junk drawer, catch-all, or whatever you call your special place for crap.

The junk drawer is the ultimate form of procrastination."Because I don't want to take the time to find a place for this, I'll just throw it in here and never use it again." For that very reason, the last place most people want to turn to when decluttering is their junk drawer.

For some, the drawer is an actual drawer, usually in the kitchen. For others, it might be a junk shelf, box or special area where all the junk winds up.

If you can, after reading this chapter, put aside 10 minutes and take care of your junk drawer. There is a reason it's called a junk drawer. You put stuff in there because it has no where else to go. The junk in there means less to you than anything in your house. That's why it's a mess and that is why it is hidden.

Try this simple test to see how important the things in your junk drawer are to you. Stand by your drawer without opening it and name 10 things inside. If you don't remember what's in there, that is a clear sign that you can live without it.

Conquer your junk drawer once and for all (any of these methods will work)

THE TABLE TOP METHOD

Dump your junk drawer onto your kitchen table. Dump it right in the middle of the kitchen table. Eat dinner around it. If all that junk enhances your meal and makes you feel good, load the junk back in the drawer and put it away. Even though you might not be completely aware of it, that feeling you have at the dinner table, surrounded by junk, is exactly how part of you feels about the junk drawer. Even though it's behind closed drawers, it takes up space in your mind.

HIDE IT

Dump the contents of your junk drawer into a bag or box. Label and hide it for 30 days. If you don't miss it, dump it. No peeking to remember what you might have forgotten.

DUMP IT

Take a leap of faith and be confident that there isn't buried treasure in the drawer. (There isn't) Dump it or donate it and be done with it once and for all.

SORT IT

If you are looking for gentler method, this is for you. Schedule an hour, turn on some calming music and sort through the junk drawer. Give each thing a proper place. If it doesn't have one, let the item go.

1. If you are worried about what to do with your junk, read Does Decluttering Help the Environment.

2. If you think because you sew, scrapbook or have another artistic hobby that you need a junk drawer, you don't.

3. If you think you don't have time to conquer your junk drawer, think of it this way, if you take 10 minutes after reading this chapter and handle it, you will never have to spend time reading or thinking about a junk drawer again. This is going to actually save you time.

Junk attracts junk and clutter attracts clutter. If that wasn't the case, your junk drawer wouldn't be so full. If you want more clutter, keep it up. If you want more time, space, and peace, you know what to do.

Quick Review: Do not waste time organizing your junk drawer. Get rid of it completely.

Chapter 12

DESKS & OFFICE SPACE

One of the most amazing things about decluttering your work space is the profound peace and focus you find once you're done. We often don't realize how much of a visual distraction clutter can be.

Look around your work space: are there lots of papers, posters/flyers/memos, Post-Its, phone messages, folders, office supplies, tools, notebooks, knickknacks, photos, other miscellaneous things? These all require your attention, even if you don't realize it.

Now imagine a space that just has the tool you need right now—a computer or a pen and notebook, maybe. Nothing else but clear space. You're able to find focus while keeping a peace of mind most people don't have during the workday.

Creating a clutter-free work space takes four steps: 1) getting rid of extra stuff you don't use; 2) finding a place for things you do use, preferably out of sight; 3) setting up a simple file system; and 4) stripping away distractions on your computer.

1. Eliminating the unnecessary

Starting with the top of your desk, then working through one drawer at a time, then moving to walls, floors, and other spaces in your office or work space, start tossing or boxing anything you don't use on a regular basis. Don't keep things "just in case" or for sentimental value. Be ruthless— everything you keep must be absolutely necessary, or it will be wasted distraction.

2. Find a hidden home

Whatever is left needs to find a permanent home. This "home" is the place where you'll always keep it when it's not in use. Try to find an out-of-sight home for almost everything—drawers, cabinets and closets are best. If it's out of sight, it won't distract you. If you don't have enough space in drawers, cabinets and closets, get rid of more stuff until you do. Then get rid of more stuff so you have a surplus of space. The only things that should be in sight are things you use throughout the day—the most-needed tools. The fewer the better. Try to create an uncluttered, distraction-free space.

3. Set up a simple folder system

Sometimes our papers pile up high because we don't have good places to put them. Create some simple folders with labels for your major types of paperwork. Put them in one spot. Your system doesn't have to be complete, but keep some extra folders and labels in case you need to quickly create a new file.

Also learn to file quickly. Once you've created your simple filing system, you just need to learn to use it regularly. Take a handful of papers from your pile, or your inbox, and go through them one at a time, starting from the top paper and working down. Make quick decisions: trash them, file them immediately, or make a note of the action required and put them in an "action" file. Don't put anything back on the pile, and don't put them anywhere but in a folder (and no cheating "to be filed" folders!) or in the trash/recycling bin.

4. Distractions on the computer

If you use the computer regularly, distractions on the computer are just as bad as distractions in the rest of the work space. First, create a "temp" folder and put all the files on your desktop into this folder. Get into the habit of saving things in this folder rather than the desktop. Use a launcher program like Launch Bar (Mac) or Launchy (Windows) to launch your programs and files—it's quicker and less messy than launching them from your desktop. Turn off all notifications if possible—calendar, email, Twitter and other reminders that keep you from doing the work you want to focus on. And close your browser if possible while you work on the important stuff.

Notes on Decluttering Papers

If you have lots of papers in your profession, it can be a tough area to tackle. Start with getting rid of as much as possible. It's always better to simplify than to organize. Be ruthless—if you don't really need it, if you can get it elsewhere, get rid of it.

If you're just not sure, keep them in a "maybe" box or two that you can put in storage. It's a good way of feeling safe about decluttering, but you'll find that you don't need the maybe box after awhile.

Digitize just about everything. All records, professional correspondence, and research can be kept online. When people send you paper stuff, request that they do it digitally. The few who can't, you can scan.

When it's online, you don't really need to organize—just tag things by topics, and you'll easily find it by searching. Google Docs, Evernote, Pinboard and other similar tools are great for this.

Chapter 13

KITCHEN

The kitchen is for preparing and eating food, but it is also the place where your family gathers during other times of the day. When you are entertaining, guests will often end up in the kitchen enjoying your company. Wouldn't it be nice to stop organizing this central location and keep it clutter free?

Stores like Ikea and Target can make it almost irresistible not to fill your kitchen with matching gadgets and tools. Resist! Seriously, how many sets of measuring cups, wine glasses, mixing bowls or wooden spoons can you use at one time. To determine what you really need in your kitchen, try one of the following action plans.

Action Plan #1

1. Empty your kitchen by moving everything into a nearby room. When you are done, it should be as empty as the day before you moved in.

2. Clean your kitchen. Get it all – cabinets, floor, counter tops, sink, windowsills, and windows.

3. Don't forget the inside of your stove and refrigerator.

4. Once the room is spotless, move in it. Walk around, sit down, stand up, and see how the clean, clear space feels. Do not move to the next step until you fully appreciate the emptiness of the space and how that allows you to think more clearly.

5. Now it's time to decide what to bring back into the room. Don't put anything on the counter top unless you use it frequently. If you only use your blender once a month, it doesn't get a spot on the counter.

6. Dump the stuff you never use. If you have a George Foreman grill stuffed in the back of a cabinet, but you don't eat meat anymore, it's time to let the grill go! If the rice cooker you bought is still in the box, sell it or give it away.

7. Check your food too. Are there cans of soup you bought, but never use? Check the expiration date and donate to a local food bank.

8. Box everything up that isn't going back in the kitchen and donate it.

(If it helps you to bring less into the kitchen, box everything up, seal it with packing tape and leave it in your garage or basement. If you don't miss it after 30 days, give it away.)

Action Plan #2

1. Follow steps 1–4 above.

2. Do not bring anything into your kitchen until you are going to use it. If you can live with the clutter in the other room for a week or longer, you will really understand how little you actually need. If you haven't brought something into the kitchen after two weeks, let it go.

3. Box everything up that isn't going back in the kitchen and donate it. (If it helps you to bring less into the kitchen, box everything up, seal it with packing tape and leave it in your garage or basement. If you don't miss it after 30 days, give it away.)

You can apply these steps to any room in your house. It is important to physically remove the things that you don't need, but think you want, for at least 30 days to see if you really do want them in the house. You will likely forget all about that vase that sat empty on your windowsill or the three extra whisks or wooden spoons cluttering up your drawers.

Imagine baking bread without having to move fifty things off the counter or inviting friends over to share a bottle of wine without having to spend an hour "picking up."

Chapter 14

BEDROOM

A calm space is important, especially in the bedroom. Your bedroom is the most personal space in your home. Make it the kind of space you look forward to starting and ending each day.

Your bedroom should be for only three things: relaxing, sleeping and sex. (not necessarily in that order) You might do other things in your bedroom like get dressed or read, but your bedroom is your sanctuary. If it's filled with piles of bills, a computer, or TV, the space becomes more like an office or game room.

After you remove distractions and other items that do nothing but collect dust, consider the following bedroom trouble spots.

Television

TV is a distraction anywhere in your home, but especially in the bedroom. Studies show that couples with a TV in the bedroom have less sex. Watching TV while dosing off can also lead to sleep disruption.

Laundry

When your laundry basket is full of dirty clothes, wash them. When clothes are clean, put them away instead of storing them on top of your dresser or on the floor.

Make your bed

The bedroom is dedicated to your bed. The bed is often the first thing you see and think about when you walk in the room. Keep it tidy to set the tone for the rest of the room. If your bed is nice and neat, you will want the rest of the room to look good too.

Pillows

If you spend more time moving decorative pillows on and off your bed than you do actually making your bed, it might be time to consider fewer pillows. Make sure any decorative item adds value to your life. If it doesn't, get rid of it.

Books

How many books are on your nightstand right now? How many books can you read at a time? You don't need a reminder of every book you want to read next to your head when you fall asleep.

Patterns

There are endless color schemes and patterns for bedding and curtains. Keep it simple. Remember this is where you fall asleep and wake up. Choose calm over chaotic.

Accessories

There is no need to fill empty surfaces for the purposes of decorating. Appreciate the empty space and the time you would have spent dusting.

Waking up to room full of clutter can sap your energy for the day and going to sleep in a messy, noisy room can disrupt your sleep. Keeping your bedroom clutter free will help you feel relaxed in the evening and refreshed in morning.

Chapter 15

Kid's Stuff

Every parent will tell you that being a clutter-free parent is an oxymoron. Kids come with more stuff than anything else in your life.

In some ways this is true, but it's definitely possible to live with less stuff. And teaching your kids about clutter, and the values that lead to buying too much, is one of the most valuable educations you can give them.

We're going to break this chapter into a few parts: 1) getting your kids on board; 2) having fun decluttering; 3) dealing with problem areas; and 4) teaching kids long-term habits.

1. Getting your kids on board

You can drag your kids kicking and screaming into your new clutter-free life, crying as you get rid of all their toys, but it's so much easier if they're on board with the changes. If they're old enough to have discussions, start talking to them about stuff, and why too much is not healthy. Talk to them about how it's hard to play with stuff if you can't even find it. Show them your decluttering efforts in other areas of the house, let them help, and show them how nice things are when they're clutter-free. It's an ongoing discussion, and kids won't get it right away. It takes them time, and you have to be patient, but the sooner you start the discussion the better. It's best if you can give them their space to have clutter, especially at first, as you declutter the rest of the house. In the long run you might consider letting them just keep their space cluttered if they aren't on board—at least it's limited damage.

2. Having fun decluttering

If and when you're ready to declutter the kids' stuff, get them to help (if they're old enough). Make it fun! You can turn decluttering into a game:

- Make it a challenge to find things they haven't played with in a long time. Put those things in a box.

- Look at their things and try to imagine who would love having the

toys or clothes, and talk about how much fun it would be to give these things as presents or donate it to a good charity.

- Make it a race—you do one area, the child can do another equal area, and see who can sort their area first into three piles (love & keep, donate, or "maybe" storage).

- Tell them if you can declutter their room, you'll have space to build a cardboard fort or castle or a tent.

- Tell them you're going to work together to sell their excess stuff, and use the proceeds to buy ice cream or go to a fun park or something. Or raise money for their next computer.

- Give points for everything they put into the donate boxes, and subtract points for everything they keep. Points buy ice cream or something like that.

These are just a few ideas—you might find your own fun ways of decluttering with your kids.

3. Dealing with problem areas

Some things are tougher to declutter than others. Here are a few ideas for some common problem areas:

- Gifts. If your child received gifts from loved ones, giving the gifts away might be a sensitive issue. But this is a good time to talk about how getting a gift is wonderful, but it shouldn't obligate you to keep an object for life. If it did, you'd end up with a ridiculous amount of stuff you couldn't ever part with.

- School papers and artwork. Report cards, significant papers and projects from school, artwork the child did at home or school . . . these are all valuable, and you might want to save them . . . but they can accumulate quickly into huge piles. Take photos of each, and save them in digital photo albums on your computer (and back them up online). Create a space like a bulletin board area for the most recent awesome pieces of artwork.

- Baby stuff. Babies come with a whole host of gadgets and gear these days—three kinds of strollers, a carrier, a sling, a carseat, a rocker, a walker, a swing, a changing pad, a changing table, a baby bath, musical toys, four diaper bags, and on and on. But our parents didn't have all this stuff. Learn to be a minimalist parent by going without it if it wasn't around 50 years ago. Parents have survived for millenia without all that gear, and so can you. Also, if your baby has outgrown the stuff, get rid of it—don't keep it "just in case" you have another baby. You can always get the essentials (and they are very few) from Craigslist or a thrift shop.

- Legos and games. Ziplocks and plastic containers are your friends. Whittle everything to a minimum, and then keep it organized so it's not all over the place.

4. Teaching kids long-term habits

Decluttering a room isn't the finish line—it's only the start. Things will get just as bad very quickly if new habits aren't learned.

- Teach your kids where things belong. If you teach your kids where things go, and start teaching them the habit of putting them there, you'll go a long way to keeping your house uncluttered. Of course, they won't learn the habit overnight, so you'll have to be very very patient with them and just keep teaching them until they've got it. And better yet, set the example for them and get into the habit yourself.

- Pick up after making a mess. Don't be a Nazi parent and require everything be perfectly spotless all the time, but you can make a game of cleaning up (with a clean-up song! "Clean up, clean up, everybody everywhere!") after they've made a mess. Teaching this habit will save you lots of headaches. Baskets for storing toys make cleaning up easy.

- Declutter on birthdays and Christmas. If they normally get a crapload of toys on special occasions, declutter before those occasions so that you'll have room. Also, if they get items anytime during the year, take out one or two items to make space for the new item.

- Finding alternatives to buying. If your kid wants to buy something, teach them to think of alternatives first. Can you make it instead? Can you reuse or recycle other items? Can you borrow it or find someone who isn't using theirs? Can you find it in a thrift shop or on Craigslist or Freecycle? Can you borrow it from the library or other lending service? Can you rent it? Make buying it, especially new, the last alternative.

Chapter 16

CLUTTER-FREE EXPERIMENTS

Becoming clutter free is a process that is different for everyone. Your commitment to living with less, who you live with, and how much stuff you have all contribute to how fast or slow you go. Choose slow, deliberate change over radical action.

There are experiments that can help kick start your journey or add momentum to your commitment.

100 Thing Challenge

Live with only 100 personal items.

Dave Bruno, The 100 Thing Challenge founder, says, "The goal of the 100 Thing Challenge is to break free from the confining habits of American-style consumerism. A lot of people around the world feel "stuck in stuff." They feel like their closets and garages are too full of things that don't really make their lives much better. But how to get unstuck?

- Reduce (get rid of some of your stuff)

- Refuse (to get more new stuff)

- Rejigger (your priorities)

I totally believe that living without an abundance of personal possessions for an extended period of time is the first
step we ought to take in order to realize that we don't need
ever-more stuff. If you do this—if you will give up your stuff
for a while—I am sure you'll never go back. You'll spend
the rest of your life creating a more valuable life, instead
of wasting your money and time on stuff. You will be glad.
And best of all, the people around you will be blessed by
your efforts to prioritize more meaningful pursuits."

http://guynameddave.com/100-thing-challenge/

Project 333

For three months, dress with 33 items or less.

Attack the clutter you wear every day. How many times
have you looked in your closet and thought, "I have nothing
to wear." The fast and furious answer is to run out and
buy something new and stuff it in your already overstuffed
closet.

Instead, try dressing with less.

- **When:** Every three months (It's never too late to
  start so join in anytime!)

- **What:** 33 items including clothing, accessories, jewelry, outerwear and shoes.

- **What not:** these items are not counted as part of the
  33 items – wedding ring or another sentimental piece
  of jewelry that you never take off, underwear, sleep

wear, in-home lounge wear, and workout clothing (you can only wear your workout clothing to workout)

- **How:** Choose your 33 items, box up the remainder of your fashion statement, seal it with tape and put it out of site. If after three months, you don't remember what's in the box, donate it.

- **What else:** consider that you are creating a wardrobe that you can live, work and play in for three months. Remember that this is not a project in suffering. If your clothes don't fit or are in poor condition, replace them.

theproject333.com/getting-started

One Dress Protest

If you thought 33 items were a challenge, what about one?
"One Dress Protest is me, Kristy Powell, wearing one dress for one year in order to protest the ideas and motivations behind how and why I wear my clothes. Over the year I aim to challenge the ways identity is constructed through clothing, what sustainability means for consumption, how our perception of others is so often based on external presentation, and what 'fashion' ultimately means for me going forward." – Kristy Powell, Founder of One Dress Protest.

Try the One Dress Protest for a week, a month, or even a year like Kristy.

http://onedressprotest.com/about/

One is Enough

Challenge the idea that one is not enough.

Just because you can walk into Target and buy 44 cups for $4.00, doesn't mean you should. Pens are cheap, but do you really need 10 or more in a jar on your desk. And why, if you start with 10, do you always have none by the end of the week? If you only had 1, would you take better care of it?

For the One is Enough challenge, create a kit for yourself. One dish, one cup, one bowl, one pen . . . you get the idea. Challenge the idea that one is enough. This might be a weekend experiment or maybe longer. You might find that one is not enough or that one is actually too much.

Bonus challenge: Make it a family affair. Will your husband, wife or children join you? See how it changes things in your family. Your dishwasher won't be running much.

These challenges will be learning experiences, but they should also be fun. If they become stressful, then your mind becomes cluttered and they defeat the purpose of living clutter free.

While living with less is not a competition, it can help to participate in one of these challenges. Not only will they give you direction and boundaries to consider, but you can connect with like minded people. You may never make it to 100 things in your home or 33 in your closet, but by working toward those numbers, you will find that you can live with less than you thought.

Chapter 17

SELL YOUR STUFF

There are many ways to get rid of your stuff, but if you are in debt, selling your stuff will help you declutter and pay down debt at the same time. If you have higher value items that you can live without, list them on craigslist, ebay or a local classified website. As soon as your item sells, apply the cash to debt.

While you can sell one thing at time, if you are feeling ambitious, you can organize the things you'd like to sell in a garage or unused space in your home. Once you see what you have available to sell, you may decide to have your "last yard sale ever." Yard sales are not fun or easy, but if you have plenty to sell, they can be worth the time.

If you have debt, a yard sale is a great way to pay it down. A yard sale will also speed up the process of simplifying, because you will only want to do this once.

Three steps for a successful yard sale

1. have a system

2. commit to paying off debt with *all* profits

3. immediately post high priced items that don't sell at the yard sale on craigslist, ebay or a local classified site and have a pick up service scheduled to come at the end of the sale to pick up the rest.

#2 and #3 are self explanatory, but you need a great system for the big day.

TWO WEEKS PRIOR TO YOUR YARD SALE:

- Divide & Conquer: Start three piles in your garage or an area that won't get in the way of your day to day living. Section 1: Sell, Section 2: Save (you want to save this stuff but you don't want it in your house) and Section 3: Toss (it's no good for you, or anyone else.) Up until two days before the yard sale, you are filling these sections with contents from your home, shed, garage, attic, car, yard . . . wherever you have stuff.

ONE WEEK PRIOR TO YOUR YARD SALE:

- Shine it up – clean everything up that you plan to sell and group it according to category.

- Donate everything that you don't plan to sell or save.

THREE DAYS BEFORE:

- Make your signs. These signs should be bright and well written.

- Buy water and refreshments to give away.

- Make change at the bank. Be prepared for customers to pay for $1.00 items with a $20.00 bill. Start with at least $80 in singles and $40 in fives.

- Borrow tables so you don't have to put everything on the ground.

- Make pricing signs for each category. For instance, if you are selling clothing, "$1.00 each or seven for $5.00." Encourage people to buy multiple items by offering a discount.

DAY BEFORE:

- Post yard sale announcements on free local websites.

- Get a good night of sleep.

DAY OF:

- Post signs in good locations.

- Make lemonade or fill cooler with refreshments.

- Display your "stuff." Take pride in merchandising items or style areas that look like rooms if you are selling furniture. Have sections to make it easier to shop, like children's, kitchen, outdoor, exercise.

- Work it! Be friendly and let customers know you are there to help.

- Be more flexible with pricing after 12:00 PM. Most of your business will be done by noon. People like to shop yard sales early.

- That evening, say goodbye to everything that did not sell and do not bring it back in the house. Have a pick up service coming for the leftovers asap.

- Count your money and immediately apply to debt.

Chapter 18

Resources for Donating, Selling, & Giving Stuff Away

Francine Jay, better known as "Miss Minimalist" was kind enough to compile a list of 101 ways your clutter can do good. Following is a partial list. See the complete list along with links to each organization on the original post: 101 Places Your Clutter Can do Good

General Goods

Goodwill

What they do: Help people with barriers to employment learn the skills to find competitive employment

What they need: Clothing, electronics, appliances, furniture, and more

Salvation Army

What they do: Provide community programs, homeless services, rehabilitation,

disaster relief, and other assistance to those in need

What they need: Clothing, furniture, household goods, sporting equipment, books, electronics, and more

VIETNAM VETERANS OF AMERICA

What they do: Help Vietnam-era veterans and their families

What they need: Clothing, baby items, housewares, electronics, small appliances, tools, and just about anything else

VOLUNTEERS OF AMERICA

What they do: Support at-risk youth, the frail elderly, men and women returning from prison, homeless individuals and families, people with disabilities, and those recovering from addictions

What they need: Clothing, furniture, toys, and household goods for their thrift stores

Clothing, Shoes, and Accessories

DRESS FOR SUCCESS

What they do: Provide interview suits, confidence boosts, and career development to low-income women in over 75 cities worldwide

What they need: Women's business suits and other professional apparel

CAREER GEAR

What they do: Provide underserved job-seeking men with training, career counseling, interviews, and professional clothing

What they need: Men's suits, dress shirts, ties, shoes, briefcases, and other interview-appropriate clothing

THE WOMEN'S ALLIANCE

What they do: Provide professional attire and career skills training to low income women and their families seeking self sufficiency

What they need: Women's business clothing and professional accessories

Wedding and Prom Dresses

BRIDES AGAINST BREAST CANCER

What they do: Advance the awareness of breast cancer, and operate a wishgranting service enabling patients to make special memories with their loved ones

What they need: New and used wedding gowns from 2005 to present

BRIDES ACROSS AMERICA

What they do: Provide wedding gowns to military brides in need

What they need: New or gently-used bridal gowns, not more than three years old

DonateMyDress.org

What they do: Provide special occasion dresses to girls who cannot afford them
for prom, sweet 16, quinceañera or formal events
What they need: Prom and special occasion dresses for young women

Baby and Children's Items

Project Night Night

What they do: Reduce the trauma of homeless children with Night Night Packages of childhood comforts
What they need: Stuffed animals, blankets, and children's books

SAFE (Stuffed Animals for Emergencies)

What they do: Collect items to give to children in emotional, traumatic, or stressful situations (like fires, illness, abuse, homelessness, and natural disasters)
What they need: New or gently-used stuffed animals

Loving Hugs

What they do: Send stuffed animals to children living in war zones, refugee
camps, orphanages, hospitals, and natural disaster areas
What they need: New or very gently-used stuffed animals

Electronics

WORLD COMPUTER EXCHANGE

What they do: Provide used computers and technology to schools, libraries, community centers & universities in developing countries

What they need: Computers, laptops, printers, hard drives, peripherals, software, and more

NATIONAL CRISTINA FOUNDATION

What they do: Provide computer technology to people with disabilities or economic disadvantages, to enable them to lead more independent and productive lives

What they need: Desktops, notebooks, printers, peripherals, software, and more

NATIONAL COALITION AGAINST DOMESTIC VIOLENCE

What they do: Work to eliminate domestic violence, and empower battered women and children

What they need: Used cell phones

Office and School Supplies

ILoveSchools

What they do: Match America's school teachers with donations of classroom resources

What they need: A variety of school supplies, materials, and equipment

SWAP4SCHOOLS

What they do: Match donors' "haves" with schools' "wants"
    What they need: Books, movies, and other items specifically requested by educators

THE GRAYMATTERS FOUNDATION

What they do: Support and empower people impacted by brain tumors through outreach, awareness, and assistance programs
    What they need: Stickers, postage stamps, blank or encouragement cards and envelopes

Books

INTERNATIONAL BOOK PROJECT

What they do: Promote education and literacy by sending quality used books overseas
    What they need: Textbooks, dictionaries, encyclopedias, vocational books, children's books, and more

GLOBAL LITERACY PROJECT

What they do: Foster community-based literacy initiatives throughout the world *What they need:* "We are currently most in need of Pre-K to 12th grade reading books as well as Math and science textbooks."

DARIEN BOOK AID

What they do: Send books in response to specific requests from Peace Corps volunteers, libraries and schools all over the world

What they need: A variety of new and gently-used books. Please call before shipping, to make sure your donations fit their needs

DVDs and CDs

KIDFLICKS.ORG

What they do: Create movie libraries for children's hospitals and pediatric wards across the US *What they need:* DVDs

DVDs4VETS

What they do: Provide DVDs to VA facilities for veterans in rehabilitation

What they need: DVDs and portable DVD players

DISCSFORDOGS.ORG

What they do: Sell used DVDs and CDs, and donate the proceeds to the SPCA *What they need:* DVDs and CDs

Art and Craft Supplies

THE CUREchief FOUNDATION

What they do: Bring hope to cancer patients, and people with other conditions that cause hair loss
   What they need: Cotton, flannel, or polar fleece fabric

CARE WEAR

What they do: Provide handmade baby items to premature infants in neonatal intensive care units
   What they need: Yarn, flannel, broadcloth, and other fabrics suitable for children's toys, apparel, and blankets/quilts

A LITTLE SOMETHING

What they do: Help refugee women in Denver become self-sufficient through crafting
   What they need: Leftover or unwanted beads or jewelry-making supplies, weaving fiber, knitting needles, and natural fiber yarn

Sports Equipment

SPORTS GIFT

What they do: Provide sports programs and equipment to impoverished and disadvantaged children throughout the world
   What they need: A wide variety of sports equipment; see website for details

ONE WORLD RUNNING

What they do: Provide running shoes to those in need in the US and throughout the world
What they need: New and near-new running shoes

BIKES FOR THE WORLD

What they do: Donate bicycles to developing countries, so that individuals can get to work or school, or provide health and education services to low-income rural people
What they need: Any serviceable adult or children's bicycles, as well as bike parts, tools, and accessories

Musical Instruments

MR. HOLLAND'S OPUS FOUNDATION

What they do: Keep music alive in our schools and communities by donating
   musical instruments to under-funded music programs
What they need: Gently-used band and orchestral instruments

MARCHING MOUNTAINS

What they do: Supply public school band programs in distressed counties in Appalachia with donated new and used musical instruments
What they need: Musical instruments in good working condition (mainly for marching and concert bands)

OPERATION HAPPY NOTE

What they do: Send musical instruments to deployed service men and women throughout the world

What they need: New or gently-used guitars, violins, mandolins, banjos, keyboards, horns of any kind, harmonicas, and even bagpipes

Eyeglasses

UNITE FOR SIGHT

What they do: Support eye care for patients living in extreme poverty in developing countries

What they need: New reading glasses, distance glasses, and sunglasses

ONE SIGHT

What they do: Provide free vision care and eyewear to people in need around the world (in some countries, a pair of eyewear costs more than a month's salary)

What they need: two million pairs of gently-used eyewear

NEW EYES FOR THE NEEDY

What they do: Send eyeglasses to medical missions and international charitable

organizations for distribution to the poor in developing nations *What they need:* Eyeglasses, reading glasses, sunglasses, hearing aids

Cars

BIG BROTHERS BIG SISTERS' CARS FOR KIDS' SAKE

What they do: Provide children facing adversity with strong and enduring, professionally supported one-to-one relationships that change their lives for the better

What they need: All types of vehicles, including cars, trucks, SUVs, motor homes, boats, airplanes, farm equipment, and construction equipment

HABITAT FOR HUMANITY CARS FOR HOMES

What they do: Build and rehabilitate houses for families in need

What they need: Cars, trucks, boats, RVs, motorcycles, and construction equipment

AMERICAN DIABETES ASSOCIATION

What they do: Strive to prevent and cure diabetes, and to improve the lives of all people affected by diabetes

What they need: Cars, trucks, trailers, boats, and RVs

See the complete list along with links to each organization on the original post: 101 Places Your Clutter Can do Good

You can sell your things on craigslist.org and ebay.com or give it away on freecycle.org. If you'd like to find organizations for dropping off or picking up your stuff, check out Excess Access. You can donate books to local libraries or share books on sites like Book Crossing and BookMooch. Homeless shelters welcome and depend on your food donations.

Getting rid of your stuff will benefit your life, and if you donate it to the right place, it can improve the lives of others.

Part III

MAINTAIN

enjoy your clutter-free life

Chapter 19

MY STUFF'S GONE, NOW WHAT?

If you've gone through the actions in the book so far, you should have a fairly empty house. Isn't it liberating?

But what do you do now?

Decluttering isn't a destination, it's a journey. You're never done, because you're creating a clutter-free lifestyle, and your life isn't over yet.

The first step: enjoy all the space. It's incredibly calming, peaceful, and Zen-like to live in a home with empty spaces, that isn't filled by clutter. Sit there in your new space, and enjoy it.

This is important for a couple reasons. First, you put in a lot of hard work, and you should enjoy the reward. It wasn't for nothing. You earned the right to bask in this beauty. Second, learn that this clutter-free environment is your new standard. Once you're used to this lack of clutter, you won't want to go back. You'll do the little steps required to keep it like this.

So soak in this clutter-free space. It's wonderful, and it's your new life.

The next step: consider moving to a smaller space. Whether you rent or own, you're not fixed in one place for life. You might be in a place that's too big now, because you originally had a lot more stuff. If that's the case, just let the idea of a smaller home take seed—no need to act on it right away.

A smaller space will allow you to live more frugally, have a smaller impact on the environment (less heating and cooling needed), and be easier to maintain.

And an important next step: learn to keep your living and working spaces clutter-free. Don't let the clutter back in!

It's all too easy to get the clutter back, but you don't want to waste all the work you've done. You don't want to let go of this new beautiful clutter-free environment. To keep it this way, you'll need three new habits:

1. The habit of putting things in their homes

Everything you own should have a home—if it's important enough to stay in your life, it's important enough to find a permanent spot for it. If you find things that don't have a permanent spot, take a minute to find one, and to remember where that spot is. Now form the habit of putting things back in their homes when you're done using them. This just takes a few seconds, but it results in the clutter-free life. It takes some focus and conscious effort at first to form this new habit, but a lot of repetition is your friend.

2. The habit of not shopping or acquiring stuff

Often we shop out of habit, or for entertainment, or out of impulse. But if we continue to shop or otherwise acquire things we don't need, we will just accumulate more clutter. Before you buy or otherwise get something, consider whether it's a true need, or if it's an impulse desire. Think about where you're going to put it, and what you'll get rid of to make space for it. Think about all the time and energy you'll spend maintaining it, and eventually getting rid of it. Consider all of the resources that went into its manufacture, and whether your "need" for it is worth this impact on the earth. Consider the cost, and how many hours you worked to earn that money, and whether it's worth that chunk of your life that you'll never get back. Think about how you can do without it, or whether you can borrow it or find a creative way to fulfill the need instead of buying. These are important habits to form in the coming months.

3. The habit of regularly decluttering

Even if you get decent at the above two habits, you'll need to declutter on a regular basis. Every few months I'll start weeding out stuff in my home, as it naturally accumulates in various sneaky ways. Put a decluttering date on your calendar for every three months, so you can get into this habit.

Chapter 20

Encouraging a Spouse or Children to Stay Simple

Of course, your new clutter-free home isn't just your responsibility, if you have a family. Whether you're married (or have a live-in boyfriend or girlfriend) without kids, or whether you have kids, it's going to have to be a team effort.

This can be difficult if not everyone is as enthused about being clutter-free as you are. And it will require some patience. But it's not a lost cause—if you look at it over the long term.

It's important to remember that forcing other people to do things rarely works. If you can in fact force them, it just means in their minds they are resisting or rebelling, and you have only gotten the appearance of compliance and order. In most cases, people will refuse to be forced, and will dig their heels in more.

So if forcing doesn't work, what does? Setting an example, having a conversation about why these things are important, showing how great a clutter-free life is, encouraging not by nagging or pushing but through praise and happy attention.

And make the decluttering process fun. If it's a game, it's something to look forward to.

Have fun living without shopping as well. There are tons of free but really fun things to do with your family—playing charades or board games you find at garage sales, playing ball outside, going for walks in parks, going to free or cheap museums, a trip to the library and reading sessions at home, drawing and painting and making music, creating a family blog, making home movies, acting in kid-directed short films, cooking or baking . . . the list is endless.

If you can have fun doing these things, you can show that the clutter-free life is better than one focused on buying and owning stuff.

A few other tips:

- New habits take awhile to form. Be gentle and patient, but remind your family of the new habits in a friendly way. A good idea is to create a chart for a new habit, and try to keep a streak of 30 or 60 days doing the new habit.

- Keep an ongoing dialogue. Involve your spouse and kids in any planning and decisions. Make it a team effort, not a solo one, by getting everyone's input. Talk about how things are affecting you, what problems come up, and how you can solve it as a group.

- There will be slip-ups. Don't worry about it—just learn from it. Stay positive, even if you take a few steps back from your forward progress. It takes people years to learn to live this new lifestyle, so remember that you're in it for the long-haul, and that change doesn't come overnight.

- Read books and watch films to get educated as a group. "Stuff" by Annie Leonard, Zen Habits and Be More With Less and other simplicity blogs, documentaries such as "Consuming Kids: The Commercialization of Childhood (http://www.youtube.com/watch?v=0uUU7cjfcdM), and so on.

Chapter 21

What to do With Gifts or Given Items

You might be vigilant with not bringing new clutter into
your life, and with getting rid of the excess that you accu-
mulated over the years . . . but what if other people give
you stuff? It's a clutter leak that isn't easily plugged: gift
giving, or just stuff that people give you (or your kids) on
a regular basis.

This isn't an easy problem to solve, to be honest. It's
largely out of your control, though there are some things
you could do to slow or possibly even stop the inflow of
given items.

Just be prepared to deal with this problem on a regular
basis. Be prepared to find people less cooperative than you
would like. It will take some patience on your part, some
understanding that people give you things not to frustrate
you, but because they love you. And that's a blessing.

Here's what we recommend:

- Start talking to friends, family and coworkers. And
  anyone else in your life who might give you stuff. Talk
  to them about your decluttering efforts, why you're

doing it, how you plan to change your habits and stay clutter-free.

- Ask them if you can agree not to give each other stuff. This can be a touchy subject sometimes, but if you do it in a positive way, and don't make it seem like they've been doing something you dislike, it can be done without hurt feelings. Show gratitude for past gifts, but just explain that you're trying to keep your stuff to a minimum.

- Suggest alternative gifts for your children, and for each other. Good ideas include experience gifts, consumables, gift certificates to restaurants or movies, and gift certificates to do things for each other (massages, yardwork, washing cars, cleaning house, babysitting, etc.).

- It's also good to talk about how "love" doesn't equal "buying things."

Many people are used to expressing their love by buying things for their loved ones, but there are many other ways to express love. Spending time with your loved ones is a better way, so share some good ways that people in your life can spend time with you or your family.

- Suggest a way for your family and friends to share items they're trying to get rid of. Perhaps an email list, a forum, or a Google Doc where people list items they need or don't need, similar to Freecycle.org but for your small group. This can be a way for people to give away things they don't need anymore, but without having to give them to people who don't want them.

- If people continue to give you items or gifts, be gracious and grateful. But continue to have a dialogue about clutter, possessions, and gift giving. Keep it positive and non-accusatory.

- After a good amount of these types of dialogues (several months at least), you could send out a mass email or Facebook message, letting people know that while their gifts have been appreciated, your new policy is to donate all future gifts to charity. By now, people should understand why. They'll also start to get the message with a policy announcement like this.

People might start to think you're a little odd. That's okay. They'll talk about it for awhile, and then start to accept it as just who you are. It's not a bad thing to be the person who doesn't want extra stuff.

Chapter 22

Say No Thank You to Free Stuff

Another sneaky clutter leak is getting free stuff. It's so easy to say yes to things that are free, and this free stuff can come from all kinds of unexpected places.

Some of the free stuff you might find: giveaways in an organization you're in or at work, free T-shirts or other gear in 5K races or triathlons or marathons, free T-shirts in organizations that you volunteer with, free giveaways at a shopping mall or grocery store or other public place, free promotional stuff being given out by political candidates or political parties or businesses, party favors at birthday parties or weddings or showers, free stuff from trade shows.

"No thank you" is the perfect response. While others may want to give you their promotional materials, you are not obligated to take it. You should consider that while saying "yes" and taking the items might be easier than saying "no thank you," there's much more involved later—you have to carry it home, find a place for it, take care of it, and eventually get rid of it when you realize you don't need it. And that requires throwing it in the garbage, finding a new home for it, or making a trip to a charity to donate the item.

Your time and energy and gas money are much more valuable than the small effort of saying, "no thank you." Value your life, as you are giving a piece of it away with each "free" item you accept.

Another common problem is getting something for "free" when you buy something. This is a marketing trick that works extremely well. But then you end up buying something you don't want so you can get something you don't need for "free." It's not free, and you end up spending money you didn't plan to spend. Ignore these special offers. They lead to the downfall of your checking account, and twice as much clutter in your home.

Chapter 23

Using Your Newfound Time & Space to Redefine Life

You've created empty space, both in physical space and maybe in your schedule as well.

What do you do with empty space?

You might leave it mostly empty, and put in it only that which really matters. You have an empty vessel, and with that emptiness comes a vast range of possibilities.

What do you do with that empty space? You create the life you want. The clutter-free Life can be anything you imagine it to be.

Start to imagine what your ideal day would be like. Can it involve simple pleasures, simple fitness, simple relationships?

It might involve some yoga or meditation in your new clutter-free space. It might be time with your spouse, or some playtime with the kids. It might mean some quiet reading, or reading time with kids. It might be body weight exercises, or time for a run or a walk. It might be cooking simple meals, for yourself or for friends or family. It might be gardening, carpentry, sewing, art. It might be creating of any kind.

Those are just a start to the possibilities. And these are mostly free, and require little. They don't contribute to clutter, but take advantage of the clutter-free environment.

The space you've created is yours to fill. Fill it carefully, but with joy.

About the Authors

About Leo

Leo Babauta is a simplicity blogger & author. He created Zen Habits, considered one of the Top 25 blogs in 2009 by *TIME* magazine with over 230,000 subscribers. He is also the creator of mnmlist.com and the best-selling books *focus* and *The Power of Less*. Leo is considered a leading expert on habit creation, productivity and simplicity. Leo started Zen Habits to chronicle and share what he learned while changing a number of his own habits, which include:

- Quitting smoking.

- Becoming a runner.

- Running several marathons and triathlons.

- Waking early.

- Becoming organized and productive.

- Eating healthier.

- Becoming a vegetarian.

- Tripling his income.

- Writing a novel and a non-fiction book.

- Eliminating his debt.

- Simplifying his life.

- Losing weight (more than 60 pounds).

- Writing several best-selling e-books.

- Starting a successful Top 25 blog.

- Starting a second blog for writers and bloggers.

- Creating a leading blog on minimalism.

- Living car-free.

About Courtney

Courtney Carver is the writer and founder of Be More With Less. She launched her blog in May 2010 to share a message of hope in simplicity. She left a 15 year career in sales and marketing in September 2011 to focus on writing, develop new ways to teach others to live more simply, and live a simpler life herself.

In addition to bemorewithless.com she created bemorewithless.com/business to encourage business owners and entrepreneurs to focus on the essential instead of getting lost in busy work.

Courtney was diagnosed with Multiple Sclerosis in 2006 and attributes her healthy lifestyle to simplifying every part of her life, from diet to debt. She moved from New England in 2004 to Salt Lake City where she lives with her husband, and 17 year old daughter.

www.ingramcontent.com/pod-product-compliance
Lightning Source LLC
Chambersburg PA
CBHW060951040426
42445CB00011B/1105